THE ART OF DYING

OSCAR HAHN

D0104422

SERIES: DISCOVERIES
LATIN AMERICAN LITERARY REVIEW PRESS
YVETTE E. MILLER
EDITOR

THE ART OF DYING

OSCAR HAHN

Translated by
James Hoggard

LATIN AMERICAN LITERARY REVIEW PRESS
PITTSBURGH, PENNSYLVANIA
1987

Latin American Literary Review Press publishes Latin American creative writing under the series title *Discoveries,* and critical works under the series title *Explorations.*

Translation copyright © 1988 by James Hoggard

Arte de morir was first published in 1977 in Buenos Aires by Ediciones Hispamerica.

Acknowledgment is made to the following publications where many of the translations in this volume first appeared, sometimes in forms different from those here: *Affinities, Alembic, Anthology of Magazine Verse and Yearbook of American Poetry, Cedar Rock, Latin American Literary Review, New Letters, Sam Houston Literary Review, Stardancer, Stone Country.*

Cover photograph by Gary Goldberg. Used by permission.

ISBN: 0-935480-32-3
Library of Congress Catalogue Card No.: 87-082268

This project is supported by a grant from the National Endowment for the Arts in Washington, D.C., a federal agency.

PREFACE

A saturnine power controls the narrative voice of Oscar Hahn's *Arte de morir*, and the book's frame of reference is global. Whether in the guise of oppressed or oppressor, insistently bleak subjects are presented with vitality and craft, as are the elegantly lyrical poems in the collection. Cosmopolitan in sensibility and versatile in presentation, Hahn stepped into notable light with this volume that prompted Enrique Lihn to call him "the premier poet of his generation."

Hahn was born in 1938 in Chile, and *Arte de morir* is his first sizable collection (first published in Buenos Aires in 1977). In it he gathered matter from two previous volumes and fleshed them out with more recent work. His voice is his own, though the darkness of tone in his work is not unusual. Many 20C poets and fictionists have turned to nightmarish imagery, to fractious depictions of a cracked world. In fact, since the publication of *Les Fleurs du Mal* by Charles Baudelaire in 1857, the dominant voices of Western poetry have often been dark—especially those with strongly urban associations. We should remember, however, that major voices have always embraced the gods and demigods of night; but they have cautioned us about them, too. And for good reason: horror can easily become a melodramatic veil hiding an absence of substance. Young poets especially seem drawn to the easy drama of sensationalism. In Hahn, though, we find maturity of execution, the presence of craft sustaining intensity of expression.

Even when his imagery suggests anger and outrage at injustice, his voice maintains control; and his manner of presentation is usually oblique rather than direct. In "Night Fable," for instance, he presents a lament about a youth who was tyrannized into unreasonable guilt and self-consciousness by life-denying priests and religiasts who, through blackness of soul and ritual, "shoved down in my mouth / to my soul the whole night." In "Vision of Hiroshima," he shows the terrible grotesquery of atomic warfare: headless bodies rise while hospital and heart sink down the drains; burning cinders meow like cats, buildings turn liquid, "And what will we do with so many ashes?" In "Adolph Hitler Meditates On The Jewish Problem," he gives icily threatening voice to the terrors of evil that could well leap, he implies, nightmarishly out of the past. In this poem and others, Hahn does not talk *about* his subject; he gives his subject voice. Such an approach gives the work

11.46

a sense of authority and a dimension of power that often does not occur when poets, using their own voices, list their complaints directly.

Other evidence of dehumanizing violence is seen in "Boxing Ring" and "The Shoeshine Boy's Go-Between." In the former he presents his matter from a mixed point of view: a seemingly bloodthirsty but simultaneously reflective spectator who encourages brawling while reflecting on its appeal: "Bust him, bust his brain, / black blood or white blood, / people'll get drunk on either." By joining the two usually opposed attitudes, Hahn makes his indictment inclusive rather than exclusive. It's that doubleness of approach, too, that helps make his poetic voice distinctive. In "The Shoeshine Boy's Go-Between," he shows an impoverished child realizing his own pointless mortality: "So many shoes to shine / and none to wear, / so many I bite myself / not to scream." The grace of lightness and the seriousness of weight merge in these songs, and because their points of reference often draw power from extra-personal elements, their effects are bracing rather than depressing. Hahn loses neither focus nor art in the flooded labyrinths of self.

Like his thematic ancestors—sonneteers of love, dantesque social critics, poetic dramatists and biblical exhorters—Hahn sees matters of mortality, corruption and injustice as subjects to be faced with the uneuphemized elegance of serious poetry. Composing the work in *Arte de morir*, he was following a tradition that the 20C has often forgotten: presenting the most important, most urgent concerns poetically. To use biblical figures as examples, one thinks of Isaiah and Amos and the writers of Ecclesiastes, Job and Apocalypse (also called Revelation). Just as the threat of breakage was real in their times, so it is in ours.

In his meditative descriptions, the carefulness, even quotability, of his phrasing keeps tensions and expectations alive and intensifies the impact of the work, especially at the closing points of poems: "such are the terrors / your beauty spreads in their wings" ("Ocular Landscape"); "and in bringing death to the water of life / they bring life to the waters of death" ("Geometric Water"); "shivering, puppeteers, / old drunks dance" ("The Drunk"). His sense of line is tight, but the control he has of his phrasing allows for spontaneity rather than self-consciousness of effect. Hahn obviously sees neatness of form here as generative of power rather than decorative.

Translating effectively a deeply measured voice like Hahn's is, of course, difficult. But so is most everything associated with art. Other than meaning, one keeps in mind that sonic effects in one language may be more (or less) vivid than they are in one's own. One even gets the idea that a grocery list written in one of the Romance languages is likely to have numerous rhymes in the names of the items; such would not be the case in English. The implication of such is that, because of its rarity in common discourse, rhyming in English will usually be much more dramatic in effect than it will be in some other languages, like Spanish and Italian. Granted, a lot of elegant and even spontaneous-sounding rhymed and regularly metered verse has been written in English; but even then there was usually great effort taken to disguise or hide or mute the rhymes by having them occur within enjambed phrases rather than at the close of end-stop lines.

One does, though, want to keep alive in a translation the sonic richness found in the original. If one is moving from Spanish to English, say, internal rhymes or alliterative (or assonantal or consonantal) effects can be helpful in suggesting an English equivalent for end-rhyme in the original. The parallel, of course, is not exact; but translating, like politics, is labor in the art of the possible. And again and again one is reminded of limits—one's own major among them. Alert to these matters, I forwent a drive to recreate in English the same patterns of sound Hahn used in Spanish. When appropriate, I used variations on the alliterative mode, the internal sonic connections that convey echoic effects in English but avoid the jingly effects often produced by end-rhyme. One also recognizes that because of the smaller variety of syllabic endings there will be a greater prevalence of internal rhyme in Spanish than in English. Still another point of limitation strikes a translator: expansions and contractions in the connotative possibilities of meaning.

To put these concerns more generally—but also perhaps more pointedly—I wanted what translators commonly want: for the translation, on its own, to be effective in its new language, for it to "work," as one says, whether or not one knows the original. I did, though, reject the option of using the original version as merely a skeletal framework for hanging a "new" poem on. Some wonderful works have been created that way, but here I felt an obligation to stay as close as I could to the original. One does one's best while realizing there are several ways to court transcultural muses. Like composing, translating involves an "adventure of the word," to quote a phrase (in translation) Hahn used once in a dedicatory note.

As I look back through the work in this volume, I realize again that increased familiarity with Hahn's poems increases my appreciation for their strength, for that openness of spirit—saturnine though it is—that synthesizes, through the insistent rhythms of its flow, the impulses of both lyricism and realism. In addition to moving us with the driving quality of his ideas, Hahn gives us textures in the experiences he calls to mind. His method is not statemental as much as it is recreative or evocative; and his frames of reference sail beyond self while including himself, and us, in his several points of focus.

Because of its vitality. Hahn's "art of dying" becomes an art of living; and the traditions one touches through it become a vast multicultural home: a point of origin as well as a point of destination. Hahn's attention moves from the pre-Socratic philosopher Heraclitus to a medieval lady, to Don Juan then the mask of a courtly lover, on into Allied and Axis atrocities in World War II, not to omit broken children, metaphorical city- and seascapes, apocalyptic visions and lyrical reflections. Going out of himself, he names himself; and the world he describes is large.

Table of Contents

THE ART OF DYING

Venid a la danza mortal los nacidos
Gamuzas y ojotas venid a la danza
Aquí no se inclina jamás la balanza
Lacayos y reyes lanzando bufidos
Tomados del brazo ya danzan unidos
Un ropavejero será tu pareja
Tendrás que entregarle tu carne más vieja
Y en puro esqueleto dar saltos tullidos.

Come to the deadly dance you people
In chamois and sandals come to the dance
Here the scales never tip
Taken by the arm lackeys and kings
Are roaring like hell and dancing united
An old-clothes dealer will be your partner
You'll have to give up your decrepit old flesh
And nothing but skeleton hop stiffly about

El emborrachado

Saltan los saltimbanquis
sobre los oros y los orines,
saltan los timbaleros
sobre timbales de puercoespines,
saltan titiritando
los borrachines titiriteros.

La mesa que sube a tu altura
bebiendo y bebiendo madera
es tabla de tu sepultura
y es ángel de tu borrachera.
Gotearon del techo las brujas
que están chapoteando en tu vaso:
no bebas sus negras burbujas,
te irás al cajón paso a paso.
Alzaron los duendes el vuelo
y van a empezar su trabajo,
tú quieres pisarlos, y el suelo
no está, siempre está más abajo.
Ya giran en círculos rojos
las cuatro murallas malditas,
ya giran los muebles con ojos
y tú tambaleas y gritas.
Y el vino con ropa de fraile
también es la muerte que espera
meterte borracho en el baile
que bailan allá en la huesera:

Bailan los saltimbanquis
sobre los oros y los orines,
bailan los timbaleros
sobre timbales de puercoespines,
bailan titiritando
los borrachines titiriteros.

The Drunk

Mountebanks jump
over diamonds and piss,
timpanists jump
over porcupines' timpani,
shivering, puppeteers,
old drunks, jump.

The table top rising up at you,
your face smack-dab in the wood,
is the slab of your tomb
and the angel of your binge.
The witches paddling in your glass
dropped from the ceiling:
you wouldn't drink their black bubbles,
you'll go to your coffin a step at a time.
Flying away the goblins go
on to begin their work,
you want to stomp on them,
and the floor's not there,
it's always farther down.
Already the four damned walls
in red circles spin,
now the furniture-with-eyes spins
and, staggering, you shout.
And the wine with monk's habit
is also death that's waiting
to push you drunk in the dance
they dance in the bonepit.

Mountebanks dance
over diamonds and piss,
timpanists dance
over porcupines' timpani,
shivering, puppeteers,
old drunks dance.

El Viviente

Allí estaba el Viviente, dando vueltas
la rueda del molino.
Sangre, sudor y lágrimas brotaban
de los sacos de harina.
Y negros sacerdotes con canastos
llenos de pan salieron, y volvieron
con monedas de plata, y entonaron
los cánticos gloriosos.
Y el Hombre tristemente los miraba
desde lo Alto de las aspas en cruz,
mientras el sol, violentamente rojo,
quemaba los trigales.

The Living-One

There was the Living-one
making the millwheel turn.
Blood, sweat and tears
poured from the flour sacks.
And black priests left
with bread-filled baskets,
returned with silver coins
and intoned holy canticles.
And the Man watched them sadly
from the crossed beams' Height
while the sun, violently red,
scorched the wheat fields.

Reencarnación de los carniceros

Y salió otro caballo, rojo: y al que estaba
sentado sobre éste, le fue dado quitar de la
tierra la paz, y hacer que los hombres se
matasen unos a otros.

San Juan, *Apocalipsis*

Y vi que los carniceros al tercer día,
al tercer día de la tercera noche,
comenzaban a florecer en los cementerios
como brumosos lirios o como líquenes.

Y vi que los carniceros al tercer día,
llenos de tordos que eran ellos mismos,
volaban persiguiéndose, persiguiéndose,
constelados de azufres fosforescentes.

Y vi que los carniceros al tercer día,
rojos como una sangre avergonzada,
jugaban con siete dados hechos de fuego,
pétreos como los dientes del silencio.

Y vi que los perdedores al tercer día,
se reencarnaban en toros, cerdos o carneros
y vegetaban como animales en la tierra
para ser carne de las carnicerías.

Y vi que los carniceros al tercer día,
se están matando entre ellos perpetuamente.
Tened cuidado, señores los carniceros,
con los terceros días de las terceras noches.

The Butchers' Reincarnation

And another horse left, red: and he, who
was riding this one, was charged with
removing peace from the land, and making
men kill one another.

St. John, *Apocalypse*

And I saw that the butchers on the third day,
on the third day of the third night,
began growing in the cemeteries
like misty lilies, like lichen.

And I saw that on the third day the butchers,
full of thrushes that were themselves,
flew harassed, harassed,
fevered with phosphorescent sulfurs.

And I saw that on the third day the butchers,
red like a shamed race,
rolled seven flaming dice,
hard like the teeth of silence.

And I saw that on the third day the lost
were reincarnated in bulls, pigs or rams
and grazed like animals
raised for slaughterhouse meat.

And I saw that the butchers are going to be
killing each other every third day forever.
Be careful, butchermen,
on third days of third nights.

La muerte está sentada a los pies de mi cama

Mi cama está deshecha: sábanas en el suelo
y frazadas dispuestas a levantar el vuelo.
La muerte dice ahora que me va a hacer la cama.
Le suplico que no, que la deje deshecha.
Ella insiste y replica que esta noche es la fecha.
Se acomoda y agrega que esta noche me ama.
Le contesto que cómo voy a ponerle cuernos
a la vida. Contesta que me vaya al infierno.
La muerte está sentada a los pies de mi cama.
Esta muerte empeñosa se calentó conmigo
y quisiera dejarme más chupado que un higo.
Yo trato de espantarla con una enorme rama.
Ahora dice que quiere acostarse a mi lado
sólo para dormir, que no tenga cuidado.
Por respeto me callo que sé su mala fama.
La muerte está sentada a los pies de mi cama.

Death Is Sitting At The Foot Of My Bed

My bed is undone: sheets on the floor
and blankets ready to fly off.
Death says she's going to make my bed:
I beg her — No! leave it undone.
Insistent, she says, Tonight's the time.
Settling in she says she loves me tonight.
Why would I, I reply, shaft myself?
Go to hell, she tells me.
Death is sitting at the foot of my bed.
Persistent, she's hot for me and wants
to leave me more shriveled than a fig.
I try to scare her off with a huge stick.
Now she says she wants to lie down beside me:
But only to sleep—don't worry.
I keep quiet about her bad reputation.
Death is sitting at the foot of my bed.

Palomas de la paz

De pronto las brumas rosadas, las densas brumas
corpulentas, desprendieron palomas blancas de
sus garras: dientes con alas, que en los aires
formaron la dentadura del cielo. Entonces vimos
a los dentistas nucleares blandir sus alicates
de uranio y disparar, y llover las palomas den-
tales sobre el prado luminoso de lava y zafiros.
El aullido vibrante del cielo hizo parir las vír-
genes, y nuestros rostros conocieron la caída de
la sangre celeste y el fruto de la guerra.

Doves Of Peace

Suddenly the pale red mists, the thick fat
mists opened their claws, releasing white
doves: winged teeth, sky's teeth wind-formed.
Then we saw nuclear dentists brandishing and
hurling their uranium pliers, and toothlike
doves raining on the field shining with lava
and sapphires. The roaring sky made virgins
give birth, and we saw the sky spilling blood
and the fruit of war.

Gladiolos junto al mar

Gladiolos rojos de sangrantes plumas,
lenguas del campo, llamas olorosas,
de las olas azules, amorosas,
cartas os llegan, pálidas espumas.

Flotan sobre las alas de las brumas
epístolas de polen numerosas,
donde a las aguas piden por esposas
gladiolos rojos de sangrantes plumas.

Movidas son las olas por el viento
y el pie de los gladiolos van besando,
al son de un suave y blando movimiento.

Y en cada dulce flor de sangre inerte
la muerte va con piel de sal entrando,
y entrando van las flores en la muerte.

Gladioli By The Sea

Red gladioli with bloody plumes,
tongues of the field, fragrant flames,
from the blue and gentle waves
letters come to you, pale seafoam.

Numerous epistles of pollen
float over the sails of mists
where at water's edge red gladioli
with bloody plumes beg for wives.

The waves, wind-stirred,
kiss the gladioli's stems
with a smooth, calm motion.

And into each sweet slow-blooded flower
death enters salt-skinned,
and the flowers enter death.

Fábula nocturna

Fíjense que murió la noche, fijensé,
por volar de teja en teja, fijensé,
que se cayó a la vereda, fijensé,
como gato negro muerto, fijensé.

La taparon con diarios negros, fijensé,
con plumas de ángel alquitranado, fijensé,
con negra sangre de carboneros, fijensé,
y con tinieblas llenas de ojeras, fijensé.

Después llegaron curas negros
y se ofrecieron a enterrarla,
después llegaron los caníbales
y se ofrecieron a enterrarla.
Los curas negros, donde fuera,
los caníbales en la panza.

Fíjense que murió la noche, fijensé,
se cayó como los mudos, fijensé,
que no pueden sepultarla, fijensé,
no hay ataúd para ella, fijensé.

Después volvieron esos curas
con un paquete de beatas
y me metieron en la boca
la noche toda hasta mi alma
como una hostia ennegrecida
por el negror de las sotanas.

Fíjense que ellos hallaron, fijensé,
ataúd para la noche, fijensé:
me la metieron al alma, fijensé.
Fíjensé que murió la noche, fijensé,
y la metieron en mi alma: fijensé!

Night Fable

Look how the night died, look,
flying from rooftop to rooftop, look,
it fell on the sidewalk, look,
like a black dead cat, look.

They covered it with black newspapers, look,
with a tarred angel's feathers, look,
with colliers' black blood, look,
and with smudge-bagged eyes, look.

Afterwards black priests came
and offered to bury it,
the cannibals came next
and offered to bury it.
The black priests outside,
the cannibals in their bellies.

Look how the night died, look,
it fell like the mutes, look,
that can't bury it, look,
there's no coffin for it, look.

Then those priests returned
with a crowd of pious women
and shoved the whole night down
in my mouth to my soul:
a communion wafer blackened
by the cassocks' blackness.

Look how they found, look,
a coffin for the night, look:
they put it in my soul, look.
Look how the night died, look,
and they shoved it—look!—in my soul.

Visión de Hiroshima

...arrojó sobre la triple ciudad un proyec-
til único, cargado con la potencia del
universo.

Mamsala Purva
Texto sánscrito milenario

Ojo con el ojo numeroso de la bomba,
que se desata bajo el hongo vivo.
Con el fulgor del Hombre no vidente, ojo y ojo.

Los ancianos huían decapitados por el fuego,
encallaban los ángeles en cuernos sulfúricos
decapitados por el fuego,
se varaban las vírgenes de aureola radiactiva
decapitadas por el fuego.
Todos los niños emigraban decapitados por el cielo.
No el ojo manco, no la piel tullida, no sangre
sobre la calle derretida vimos:
los amantes sorprendidos en la cópula,
petrificados por el magnésium del infierno,
los amantes inmóviles en la vía pública,
y la mujer de Lot
convertida en columna de uranio.
El hospital caliente se va por los desagües,
se va por las letrinas tu corazón helado,
se van a gatas por debajo de las camas,
se van a gatas verdes e incendiadas
que maúllan cenizas.
La vibración de las aguas hace blanquear al cuervo
y ya no puedes olvidar esa piel adherida a los muros
porque derrumbamiento beberás, leche en escombros.
Vimos las cúpulas fosforescer, los ríos
anaranjados pastar, los puentes preñados
parir en medio del silencio.

Vision Of Hiroshima

... I hurled over the triple city a unique pro-
jectile loaded with the power of the uni-
verse.

Mamsala Purva
Sanskrit millenary text

Eyeshock: the bomb itself spraying eyes
from under the living mushroom:
eyes kaleidoscoping with blind humanity's brilliance.

The elders, decapitated by the fire, scattered,
the angels, decapitated by the fire,
rammed against sulfuric horns,
the virgins, haloed radioactively, were stopped,
decapitated by the fire.
All the children dispersed decapitated through the sky.
It wasn't maimed eye or paralyzed skin
or blood over melted street that we saw:
but coupling lovers astonished,
petrified by the inferno's magnesium,
the lovers fixed on the public road,
and Lot's wife
turned into a uranic column.
The hot hospital goes through the drains,
your gelid heart goes through latrines,
they go under the beds, like cats,
green and inflamed, they go on all-fours,
cinders meowing.
The waters' vibration turns the raven white
and now you can't forget that skin stuck on the walls
because you'll drink in collapse, milk in riprap.
We saw domes phosphorescing, slow rivers
turned orange, bulging bridges
giving birth in the middle of the silence.

El color estridente desgarraba
el corazón de sus propios objetos:
el rojo sangre, el rosado leucemia,
el lacre llaga, enloquecidos por la fisión.
El aceite nos arrancaba los dedos de los pies,
las sillas golpeaban las ventanas
flotando en marejadas de ojos,
los edificios licuados se veían chorrear
por troncos de árboles sin cabeza,
y entre las vías lácteas y las cáscaras,
soles o cerdos luminosos
chapotear en las charcas celestes.

Por los peldaños radiactivos suben los pasos,
suben los peces quebrados por el aire fúnebre.
¿Y qué haremos con tanta ceniza?

The harsh color tore out
the heart of its own objects:
red blood, rosy leukemia, festering sore,
driven mad by the fission.
Oil ripped the toes from our feet,
chairs smashed against windows
tossed on the eyes' stormy currents,
liquified buildings came gushing
past headless treetrunks,
and among husks and milky ways,
suns or luminous pigs
paddling in celestial pools.

Footsteps climb the radioactive stairs,
broken ridges rise through the funeral air.
And what will we do with so many ashes?

Cuadrilátero

A los que vengan a golpearse
sin conocerse, sin odiarse,
el cuadrilátero ya espera.

Blanco con blanco frente a frente,
negro con negro frente a frente,
y blanco y negro y negro y blanco
danzan la danza de la muerte.
Pégale, pégale en la cara,
pégale, pégale en la mente,
con sangre negra o sangre blanca
se embriagarán igual las gentes.
Dale más fuerte sobre el tórax,
dale más duro sobre el vientre,
bailen al son de los aplausos,
bailen la danza de la muerte

A los que vengan a golpearse
sin conocerse, sin odiarse,
el cuadrilátero ya espera.

Boxing Ring

Let them come beat each other
without knowing each other, without hating each other,
the ring's ready.

White with white face to face,
black with black face to face,
and white and black and black and white
dance the dance of death.
Bust him, bust him in the face,
bust him, bust his brain,
black blood or white blood,
people'll get drunk on either.
Hit him harder in the chest,
hit him harder in the belly,
dance to the sound of applause,
dance the dance of death.

Let them come beat each other
without knowing each other, without hating each other,
the ring's ready.

El muerto en incendio

Entramos en un bosque furiosamente quemado, violentamente
   abrasado.

Extraños árboles de pie nos ofrecieron frutos llamados ascuas,
   flores llamadas brasas.

De estos árboles o frutos o flores, la quemadura es la sustancia,
   el ojo en llamas:

ascuas florales, quemaduras arbóreas, brasas frutales.

Y había flamencos de carbón que cantaban pavesas.

Sólo al muerto en incendio le es dado ver esas canciones.

The Flaming Corpse

We entered a furiously scorched, violently burned forest.

Strange seedlings offered us fruits called embers,
    flowers called cinders.

From these trees or fruits or flowers, the burn is the
    essence, the eye aflame:

floral embers, arboreal burns, fruit-bearing hot coals.

And there were carbon flamingoes singing cinders.

Only the flaming corpse is allowed to know those songs.

Cafiche de la muerte

Como carne de cóndores hirvientes
o de tordos quemados, como cresta,
del rojo al negro se cambió la fiesta
y en silencio se fueron los clientes.
Se nos vació no más todo el prostíbulo,
se vaciaron las camas y los bares,
y todas las que estábamos de a pares
sollozamos de a una en el vestíbulo.
Por el pasillo viene la señora,
siempre tan maternal, siempre a la hora,
con su taza de té y un trago fuerte.
Para qué te moriste, desgraciado.
Mira mi pobre cuarto desolado,
tipo traidor, cafiche de la muerte.

Death's Pimp

Like condor meat boiling or thrushes charred,
like cock's comb, the party turned black from red
and the customers silently left.
Immediately we evacuated the whorehouse,
the beds and bars emptied,
and those of us once couples
sobbed in the lobby as one.
Always so maternal, always on time,
madam comes through the corridor
with her cup of tea and strong drink.
What did you die for, wretch.
Look at my poor desolate place,
you bastard, you damn death's pimp.

Fotografía

... alguien desarrollaba
el negativo de su existencia

                    Braulio Arenas

En la pieza contigua,
alguien revela el negativo de tu muerte.
El ácido penetra por el ojo de la cerradura.
De la pieza contigua, alguien entra en tu pieza.
Ya no estás en el lecho:
desde la foto húmeda miras tu cuerpo inmóvil.
Alguien cierra la puerta.

Photography

... someone unrolled
the negative of his existence.

Braulio Arenas

In the next room
someone develops your death's negative.
Acid penetrates the closure's eye.
From the next room, someone enters your room.
You're not in your bed now:
from the wet photo you look at your motionless body.
Someone shuts the door.

Don Juan

Todas estas mujeres que rodean
el lecho donde yazgo cada día
son un coro de velas carnosísimas
pero se van en fila retirando
y estoy solo otra vez en el espacio
del mundo y ahora pasan lentamente
por mi lecho de nuevo pero no
aunque estás a mi lado respirando
con tantas bocas tantos ojos múltiples
locamente y yo miro el cielo raso
y el lecho donde yazgo cada día
mientras todas las bellas van poniendo
flores blancas sobre este pobre cuerpo
que me cubren de arena que me cubren
de arena blanca y respirar no puedo
en mi lecho caliente circundado
por mujeres que rezan y que lloran

Don Juan

All these women circling the bed
where each day I lie
are a choir of big fat vigilants
but they withdraw in file
and again I'm in world-space alone
and now again they pass
slowly by my bed but not
if you're at my side breathing
madly many-mouthed many-eyed
and I look at the flat ceiling
and the bed where each day I lie
while all the beauties pass
putting white flowers on my poor body
and covering me with sand covering me
with white sand and I can't breathe
surrounded in my hot bed by women
who mutter prayers and mourn

Canción de Blancaflor

Ci-gît la belle Blanchefleur
à qui Flore eut grand amour.

Anónimo, siglo XII

El alma de Blancaflor
herida flota en el río
en el río del amor

Cantaron mágicamente
las estatuas Y las aves
sollozaron en la fuente

Callaron los cortesanos
Una bandada de halcones
miedosa huyó de sus manos

La que compartió su suerte
de amor con el ser amado
a solas va con su muerte

Luminosa de rocío
yace cubierta de rosas
en aguas muertas de frío

El alma de Blancaflor
herida flota en el río
en el río del amor

Song Of Blanchefleur

Here lies the beautiful Blanchefleur
for whom Flore had a great love.
Anonymous, 12C

The soul of Blanchefleur
floats wounded in the river
in the river of love

The statues sang magically
and the birds
sobbed in the fountain

The courtiers were silent
A frightened flock of falcons
fled from their hands

She who shared her passion
with her beloved
goes into death alone

Shining with dew
she lies covered with roses
in cold dead waters

The soul of Blanchefleur
floats wounded in the river
in the river of love

La última cena

La corrupción se sienta
sobre los limpios cuerpos
con servilleta y tenedor y cuchillo.

The Last Supper

Decay settles
on the clean bodies
with napkin and fork and knife.

Invocación al lenguaje

Con vos quería hablar, hijo de la grandísima.
Ya me tienes cansado
de tanta esquividad y apartamiento,
con tus significantes y tus significados
y tu látigo húmedo
para tiranizar mi pensamiento.
Ahora te quiero ver, hijo de la grandísima,
porque me marcho al tiro al país de los mudos
y de los sordos y de los sordomudos.
Allí van a arrancarme la lengua de cuajo:
y sus rojas raíces colgantes
serán expuestas adobadas en sal
al azote furibundo del sol.
Con vos quería hablar, hijo de la grandísima

Invocation To Language

I wanted to speak with you, big shot.
You've already worn me out
with all your indifference and distance,
with your signs and your symbols
and your wet whip
tyrannizing my thought.
I want to see you now, big shot,
because I'm marching right into the country
of the mutes and the deaf and the deaf-mutes.
They're going to tear out my tongue there:
and its red hanging roots, exposed,
will be preserved in salt
in the furious sunscourge.
I wanted to speak with you, big shot.

Agua geométrica

Círculos dan las aguas temerarias,
estas aguas sin duda inteligentes,
a la lluvia de fúnebres tangentes
y de cuerdas y cuerdas sanguinarias.
Dan a las bisectrices funerarias
ángulos estas aguas transparentes,
lados a las guadañas congruentes,
estas aguas sin duda solitarias.
Crecida el agua por la lluvia, dados
líquidos cuerpos a la mar crecida,
tangentes, cuerdas, bisectrices, lados,
llueven y llueven cada vez más fuerte,
y al darle muerte al agua de la vida
les dan vida a las aguas de la muerte.

Geometric Water

Circles turn the stormy waters,
these surely sentient waters,
into a shower of bleak tangents
and lines and bloody lines.
These transparent waters,
these surely solitary waters,
bring angles to bleak bisectors,
sides to congruent scythes.
Liquid bodies given over to seaswell,
rain raising the water,
tangents, lines, bisectors, sides pouring
and each time pouring more furiously,
and in bringing death to the water of life
they bring life to the waters of death.

Fragmentos de Heráclito al estrellarse contra el cielo

Heráclito vivía en un río de Efeso
encerrado en la placenta del sueño
lejos de los dormidos de la ribera

Heráclito tenía la barba luenga
y la lengua larga para lamerte mejor

No nos bañamos dos veces en el mismo río
No entramos dos veces en el mismo cuerpo
No nos mojamos dos veces en la misma muerte

A bordo de un tonel sube el Oscuro
en dirección a los rápidos rápidos
a contracorriente de Parménides
y desemboca en la Biblioteca de Londres
con la barba más negra y ancestros de aire

Heráclito vivía en un río de Efeso
pero no se bañaba dos veces en el mismo río
Se bañaba en la catarata de un ojo
se bañaba en su acuoso cuerpo
y rielaba fluía y ondulaba

Parménides vivía en un bloque de hielo
y se bañaba siempre en el mismo bloque

El que se purifica manchándose con sangre
el que se limpia el barro con barro
en este punto trata de retornar contradiciéndose
y reingresa en las llamas acuáticas
en las aguas flamígeras que flamean

Fragments of Heraclitus To Hurl Against The Sky

Heraclitus lived in a river of Ephesus
locked in sleep's placenta
far from those sleeping on the bank

Heraclitus had a long beard
and a long tongue to lick you with

We do not bathe in the same river twice
We do not enter the same body twice
We are not engulfed twice by the same death

Aboard a barrel Darkness rises
toward the rapid rapids
in Paramenides' countercurrent
and flows into the London Library
with blacker beard and airy ancestors

Heraclitus lived in a river of Ephesus
but did not bathe in the same river twice
He bathed himself in the cataract of an eye
he bathed himself in his watery body
and glistening and undulant flowed

Parmenides lived in a block of ice
and always bathed himself in the same block

He who purifies himself by staining himself with blood
he who cleans mud off himself with mud
ends up contradicting himself
and re-enters the watery flames
in the blazing flaming waters

A grupas da la luz monta el Oscuro
en dirección al gran Fuego celeste
a la velocidad del sentimiento
de los que se aman a primera vista
y se destroza en astillas de hielo
contra los muros del espacio finito
embarrado de estiércol y fango estelar

Si Heráclito no tuviera hidropesía
las clínicas se llenarían de agua
las camas blancas de arroyos enfermos
si Heráclito no tuviera hidropesía

Y en el Corral de las Constelaciones
los animales luminosos disputan
los desperdicios de su cuerpo encallado
La Osa chupa la miel de sus vértebras
el Pez desgarra sus carnes con algas
y el Can entierra en el cielo sus huesos

Heráclito vivía en el éter del Cosmos
y era una tempestad de aerolitos
en dirección a los Mares terrestres

Heráclito tenía el alma seca
y el vino triste y un aire soñoliento

Darkness rides the croups of light
toward the great celestial Fire
with the quickness of feeling
of those who love at first sight
and shatters itself into ice-chips
against the walls of finite space
smeared with dung and stellar slime

If Heraclitus had not had dropsy
the clinics would be flooded with water
the white beds with diseased streams
if Heraclitus had not had dropsy

And in the Corral of the Constellations
the luminous animals fight
for his broken body's remains
The Bear sips honey from his vertebrae
the Fish rips his flesh with seaweed
and the Dog buries his bones in the sky

Heraclitus lived in the Cosmos' ether
and was a meteor shower
falling toward terrestrial Seas

Heraclitus' soul was dry,
his wine sad, and his air sleepy

Correveidile del lustrabotas

Correveidilero corre,
correveidilero ve.
Corre, ve y diles que vengan
a llorar junto a mis pies.

Tanto lustrar y lustrar
y no tener qué ponerse,
tanto tener que morderse
por no empezar a gritar:
que ya basta, que ya basta,
que voy a emplear la pasta
con que lustro los zapatos
para escribir en los muros:
Se nos terminó el mal rato.

DICE LA MUERTE:
—No pierdas pues la ocasión,
muchacho, que voy a darte.
Ahora yo voy a lustrarte:
Coloca un pie en el cajón.

Tú te quisiste lustrar
los zapatos con la muerte
y al fin te quedaste inerte
mirándole su mirar.
Que es de un hielo negro dicen
las viejas que tienen pacto
con el diablo, y en el acto
te maldicen, te maldicen.

—Ya puse un pie en el cajón,
caballero, el pie derecho.
—Coloca ahora el izquierdo,
lustrabotas, y está hecho.

The Shoeshine Boy's Go-Between

Busybody run,
busybody see.
Run, see and tell who'd come
to weep at my feet.

So many shoes to shine
and none to wear,
so many I bite myself
not to scream:
that's enough, that's enough,
I'm going to take the paste
used for shining shoes
to write on the walls:
The bad time's over for all.

DEATH SAYS:
—Don't lose your chance, my boy,
I'm giving you this one.
Now put your foot on the box.
I'm going to polish you now.

You were about to shine
the shoes with death
but stood there sluggish
staring back at him.
It's like a black frost
say old women in league
with the devil, and instantly
they curse you, they curse you.

—I've placed now one foot on the box,
sir, the right foot.
—Now put the left one there,
shoeshine-boy, and it's done.

Cúidate del empujón,
hijo mío, cuidaté,
Que si pones los dos pies
te irás por el socavón.

—Pasta negra, pasta negra
solamente tiene usted.
—Yo lustro sólo con negro
de la cabeza a los pies.
—Y qué precio he de pagar:
Mire mi ropa raída.
—Yo cobro sólo al contado:
mi sueldo es tu propia vida.
—Su cajón es de difunto,
su trapo es una mortaja.
—Mi tinta es tu misma sangre
y hay un abismo en mi caja.

Correveidilero corre,
correveidilero ve.
Corre, ve y diles que vengan
a llorar junto a mis pies.

Watch out for the shove,
my son, watch out.
If you set both feet there
you'll drop through the cave.

—Black paste, black paste,
that's all you have.
—From head to toe
I polish only with black.
—And how much do I have to pay:
look at my worn-out clothes.
—I just take cash:
your life's my pay.
—Your box is for a corpse,
your rag is a shroud.
—My dye is your own blood,
an abyss lines my box.

Busybody run,
busybody see.
Run, see and tell who'd come
to weep at my feet.

Paisaje ocular

Si tus miradas
salen a vagar por las noches
las mariposas negras huyen despavoridas:
tales son los terrores
que tu belleza disemina en sus alas.

Ocular Landscape

If your glances
go wandering through the nights
black butterflies flee horrified:
such are the terrors
your beauty spreads in their wings.

O púrpura nevada o nieve roja

Está la sangre púrpura en la nieve
tocando a solas llantos interiores
al soplo de memorias y dolores
y toda la blancura se conmueve
Fluyendo van en ríos de albas flores
los líquidos cabellos de la nieve
y va la sangre en ellos y se mueve
por montes de silencio silbadores
Soñando está la novia del soldado
con aguas y más aguas de dulzura
y el rostro del amado ve pasar
Y luego pasa un río ensangrentado
de blanca y hermosísima hermosura
que va arrastrando el rostro hacia la mar

Either Snowy Blood Or Red Snow

Purple blood in the snow
draws interior tear-floods in private
when memories and griefs strike
and soil the whiteness
The snow's liquid hairs flow
in rivers of white flowers
and the blood stirred in them
whistles through the mountains' silence
With waters, with sweeter waters
the bride dreaming of the soldier
sees her lover's face passing,
the blood-stained river passing
with a white and startling beauty
washing the face to the sea

Canis familiaris

Llegará. Siempre llega. Siempre llega puntual
el sin cesar ladrido del perro funerario.
Entra por la ventana y repleta tu cuerpo
con puntiagudos ruidos.
Es una larga máquina de escribir, con cabezas
de perro como teclas. No te deja dormir
el tecleo canino de ese perro canalla.
El sin cesar ladrido del perro funerario
llegará. Siempre llega. Siempre llega puntual.

Canis Familiaris

It'll return. It always returns. Is sure to return
the funeral dog's endless barking.
It comes in through the window and crams your body
full of sharp noises.
It's a long typewriter with dog-headlike keys.
It won't let you sleep
that cur's canine tapping.
The endless barking of the funeral dog
will return. It always returns. Is sure to return.

Esta rosa negra

esta muerte   esta rosa negra
      a mí te debes
      y agradéceme
que cuando yo comience a morir
      tú estarás naciendo

This Black Rose

this death   this black rose
            you're in debt to me
            and should thank me
for when I begin dying
            you'll just be budding

De tal manera mi razón enflaquece

La razón de estas aguas, la perfecta
lógica de estas aguas, de esta mente
líquida, que la curva de la recta
distingue, y la sustancia, el accidente,
se desmorona cuando por su frente
oye pasar los peces funerales
y quedar en su trágica corriente,
de la nada, las huellas digitales.

In Such A Way My Reason Weakens

The order of these waters, the perfect
logic of these waters, of this liquid
understanding that differentiates curve
from straight line, and essence,
accident, falls apart when
it hears funeral fish passing
and stopping in their tragic running,
from nothing, my moving hand

Para darle cuerda a la muerte

Cuando se me alborotan los espermios,
qué veo, qué veo, digo yo:
veo a mis pescaditos navegar por los úteros,
enamorados de cuanto óvulo cae.

Winding Up Death

When the sperms arouse me
what do I see, what do I see, I say:
I see my little fish sailing through wombs,
enamored by whatever egg drops.

Velorio del angelito

Las ocho han dado y sereno,
las nueve cinco y soñando,
muriendo, las diez un cuarto,
la medianoche llorando.

Dónde está el sol, dónde el agua,
dónde el pastor y su piño.
La muerte cortaba rosas:
duerma en paz, que cortó un niño.

Mire como llora el guaina,
mire a la china, amarilla,
mire el guitarrón sin lengua:
un ángel sobre una silla.

Déjese de zancadillas,
a usted, muerte, se lo digo:
ya no le importa ni un higo
destrozarnos las rodillas.

El niño de las ovejas
que quiso cantarle a Dios
se nos voló en una cueca:
su nicho es un guitarrón.

Qué dulce el pastor escrito
por la pluma de la muerte:
en unos escribe suave
y en otros la entierra fuerte.

Las ocho han dado y sonando,
las nueve cinco rompiendo,
callando las diez un cuarto
la medianoche naciendo:
la muerte han dado y llorando,
la muerte en punto y lloviendo.

The Little Angel's Wake

Eight o'clock and clear,
nine-o-five and dreaming,
dying, ten-fifteen,
at midnight crying.

Where's the sun, where's the water,
where's the shepherd and his flock.
Death was cutting roses:
rest in peace, for he's cut down a child.

Look how the boy weeps,
look at the jaundiced little girl,
look at the soundless big guitar:
an angel on a chair.

Quit your dirty tricks,
death, I'm telling you:
it no longer matters at all
if you cut us down to our knees.

The child of the ewes
who wanted to sing to God
left us in a dance:
his niche is a big guitar.

The shepherd's so sweet
described by death's pen:
on some she writes mildly
and in others she drives it in hard.

Eight o'clock and reporting,
nine-o-five breaking,
ten-fifteen hushing
midnight being born:
death has struck, and sobbing,
death right on time, its raining.

Movimiento perpetuo

Al son de un suave y blando movimiento,
arroyos vas pisando de dulzura.
Tus pasos pisan, pasan por la oscura
región de mi memoria. Ya no siento

ni el ruido de la puerta ni el lamento
del lecho al irte. Pasa tu hermosura,
se pierde en el umbral. Tu mano pura
cerró el vestido.

            Piénsanme dormido
tus pasos. Pisan, pasan por mi mente
igual que ayer. Mi pobre sentimiento

qué solo está, qué solo estoy tendido
mirándote partir perpetuamente
al son de un suave y blando movimiento.

Perpetual Motion

With the sound of a smooth, lithe motion
you press through streams gently.
Your steps press, they pass by the dark
region of my memory. I don't hear

the door's noise now or the bed's lament
as you leave. Your beauty passes,
it's lost in the doorway. Your pure hand
fastened your dress.

        Asleep, I keep expecting
your steps. They press, they pass through my mind
as they did yesterday. I feel so alone

so alone stretched out gazing
at you leaving forever
with the sound of a smooth, lithe motion.

Ciudad en llamas

Entrando en la ciudad por alta mar
la grande bestia vi su rojo ser.
Entré por alta luz por alto amor
entréme y encontréme padecer.
Un sol al rojo blanco en mi interior
crecía y no crecía sin cesar
y el alma con las hordas del calor
templóse y contemplóse crepitar.
Ardiendo el más secreto alrededor
mi cuerpo en llamas vivas vi flotar
y en medio del silencio y del dolor
hundióse y confundióse con la sal.
Entrando en la ciudad por alto amor
entrando en la ciudad por alta mar.

City In Flames

Entering the city by high tide
I saw the great red beast
In broad daylight I entered by lofty love
I entered and found myself suffering
A red-hot sun white inside me
grew but did not grow endlessly
and the soul with hordes of heat
was cooled and seen crackling
I saw this most secret thing burning
floating around my body in bright flames
and in the middle of silence and grief
it collapsed and was mixed with salt:
entering the city by lofty love
entering the city by high tide.

Adolfo Hitler medita en el problema judío

Toma este matamoscas y extermina a los ángeles,
después con grandes uñas arráncales las alas.
Ya veo sus muñones, ya los veo arrastrarse:
desesperadamente tratan de alzar el vuelo.
Toma este insecticida. Oigo sus toses blancas
prenderse y apagarse. Una puesta de sol
o una puesta de ángeles es lo mismo sin duda
porque la noche ahora levanta su joroba
y ellos se van hundiendo lentamente en el suelo.
Levanta al pie despacio. Así mismo. Tritúralos.
Que les saquen las plumas con agua hirviendo y pongan
esos cuerpos desnudos on las fiambrerías.
Ahora me van pasando sudarios de juguete
y ataúdes con cuerda. Ahora me van pasando
las cruces más pequeñas, para que se entretengan
los infantes difuntos. Pásame el insectario,
los alfileres negros. Toma este matamoscas
y extermina a los ángeles.

Adolph Hitler Meditates On The Jewish Problem

Take this flyswatter and exterminate the angels,
then with big clawhooks root out their wings.
I see their stumps now, now I see them hauled off:
they try desperately to fly.
Take this insecticide. I hear them catching
and muffling their white coughs. A sunset
or a setting of angels is doubtless the same
because the night now lifts its hump
and they slowly sink into the ground.
Lift your foot slowly. That's it. Crush them.
Root their feathers out with boiling water and stick
those stripped bodies into lunch baskets.
Now the toy shrouds and corded coffins pass by me.
Now the smallest crosses pass by me,
so the dead infants might be amused.
Hand me the mountingboard, the black pins.
Take this flyswatter and exterminate the angels.

Elevación de la amada

Qué es el hombre para que de él tengáis memoria
Para que de ella tengáis olvidos qué es la muerte
Los dioses qué son para que de ellos tengáis angustias
Qué es la amada para que tengáis de ella insomnios

Cuál silencio puede ser más hondo
El que brilla en las llagas de la nada
O el que fulge después de tus sollozos
Como una lámpara invisible

Dulce es la aurora de las madreselvas
Dulce es
Dulce es el beso de la amada
Dulce es
Cuán dulce eres tú oh hurtadora de mi agónico sueño

Todos los adioses están escritos en el viento
Todas las palomas llevan adioses en las alas
Todos los ojos guardan un llanto no vertido
Y he aquí las palabras que no te he dicho

El amor rompe leyes
Nada contra corrientes y sus ojos escuchan
De rebeliones y quebrantos está hecho el amor

Hacia lo alto van los frutos maduros
Hacia la tierra el vuelo de los pájaros
Pero su condición no piérdese

De nosotros dos está hecho el amor

Elevation Of The Beloved

What about the man makes you remember him
What about the woman makes you forget she's death
What about the gods makes you suffer
What about your lover leaves you sleepless

Which silence is more profound
The one shining in the sores of nothingness
Or the one fleeing from your sobs
Like an invisible lamp

Dawn with honeysuckle is sweet
It's sweet
The kiss of your lover is sweet
It's sweet
You're so sweet o thief of my death-spasm dream

Every goodbye is written in wind
Every dove carries goodbye in its wings
Every eye holds an unreleased tear-flood
And here are words I haven't told you

Love breaks laws
It swims upstream and its eyes hear
Love is made from rebellions and losses

Ripe fruits grow high
Birds fly toward the earth
But love's quality's not lost

From us two love is made

El hombre

Emergió de aguas tibias
y maternales
para viajar a heladas
aguas finales
A las aguas finales
de oscuros puertos
donde otra vez son niños
todos los muertos

The Man

He emerged from tepid
and maternal waters
in order to journey
to cold final waters
To the final waters
of dark ports
where all
the dead
are children again.

El púber pálido

Los crecimientos y el espejo lampiño
que se cubre de bellos, la ciencia
del mal conocen y el parco rugido
del sexo aullador, aullador.

(Musgos llenos de miel tiene el joven,
vías lácteas de origen terrestre,
y en ellas el demonio alimenta
sus criaturas de sal celestiales.)

Los crecimientos de la edad en el cuerpo
y el sodomita de pie ante la luna,
el espectro del sexo aullador
conocen, aullador, aullador.

The Pale Pubescent

The risings and the beardless mirror
covered beautifully, they know
about evil and the muffled roar
of sex howling, howling.

(Youth has mosses full of honey,
milky ways of earthly source,
and in them the demon feeds
his salty celestial creatures.)

The body's risings at that age
and the sodomite standing before the moon,
and the howling specter of sex,
they know that, howling, howling.

La caída

De tumbo en tumbo dando bote y bote
por la escala desciende la pelota
y al dar y dar y dar ese rebote
se le va el movimiento gota a gota
De tumbo en tumbo sin cesar rebota
y rueda sin cesar de tumba en tumba
mientras el agua de la muerte brota
y su marea fieramente zumba
Subiendo va por todos los peldaños
el agua en un mortuorio crecimiento
los días y los meses y los años
Y lejos de los dóndes y los cuándos
ya van con un inmóvil movimiento
cayendo en aguas duras cuerpos blandos

The Fall

Tumbling and bouncing, bouncing and tumbling
the ball goes down the scale
and bouncing back again and again and again
its movement goes hop by hop
From bounce to bounce it keeps rebounding
rolling from bounce to bounce
while death's water gushes
and its tide fiercely hums
The water rises through all the steps
of days and months and years
in a swelling mortuary
And far from the wheres and whens
with a fixed movement soft bodies drop now
into waters that are rough

El amor

La luz que cada ciego
dejara tras lo oscuro abandonada
con duplicado fuego
enciende tu mirada
y apaga las tinieblas de la nada

Love

The forsaken light each blind one
releases beyond the dark
with doubled fire
ignites your gaze
and destroys nothing's darkness

El agua

El
agua
fluye purísima
y
descansa
La
muerte
tiene sed
fluye purísima
y
descansa
La
muerte
está bebiendo
de mi mano
y
descansa

Water

Water
flows so purely
and
rests
Death
is thirsty
flows so purely
and
rests
Death
is drinking
from my hand
and
rests

Los ropavejeros

Aquellas dulces bestezuelas de piel hundida,
con sus mandíbulas batientes y golpeantes,
en la quebrada del miedo pánico trabajan:
y hacen embudos con los uranios más envidiosos
para el vaciado de ojos y cáscaras en sacos muertos
que aquellos lentos ropavejeros llenan y cargan,
cargan y suben por las galaxias de las tinieblas
donde son una la carga humana y el cargador.

Old-Clothes Dealers

Those sweet little crushed-skin beasts,
with their flapping and rattling jaws,
work in the gorge of panicky fear: and
with the most enviable uraniums make molds
for casting eyes and hulls into faded sacks
sluggish old-clothes dealers fill and haul,
haul and lug through galaxies of darkness
where human freight and freighter are one.

La muerte tiene un diente de oro

La muerte no tiene dientes: se ríe con la encía pelada.
Y cuando muere un rico, la muerte tiene un diente de oro.
Y cuando muere un pobre, no tiene ningún diente
o le crece un diente picado. ¿Cachái, ganso?

La muerte tiene la boca
llena de muelas tristes, de colmillos cariados,
llena de jugo gástrico en lugar de saliva.

Yo tuteo a la muerte.
"Hola, Flaca, le digo, ¿Cómo estái?"
Porque todavía soy un diente de leche.

Death Has A Gold Tooth

Death is toothless and laughs bare-gummed.
But when a rich man dies, death gets a gold tooth.
Yet when a poor man dies, it has no teeth
or swells up with a tooth-ache. Get it, goose?

Death keeps the mouth
full of bad molars and decayed canines,
full of gastric juice instead of saliva.

I hail death straight on.
"Hey, Skinny, I say. How are ya?"
Because I'm still a milk-tooth.

Tractatus de sortilegiis

En el jardín había unas magnolias curiosísimas, oye,
unas rosas re-raras, oh,
y había un tremendo olor a incesto, a violetas macho,
y un semen volando de picaflor en picaflor.
Entonces entraron las niñas en el jardín,
llenas de lluvia, de cucarachas blancas,
y la mayonesa se cortó en la cocina
y sus muñecas empezaron a menstruar.
Te pillamos in fraganti limpiándote el polen
de la enagua, el néctar de los senos, ves tú?
Alguien viene en puntas de pie, un rumor de pájaros
pisoteados, un esqueleto naciendo entre organzas,
alguien se acercaba en medio de burlas y fresas
y sus cabellos ondearon en el charco
llenos de canas verdes.
Dime, muerta de risa, a dónde llevas
ese panal de abejas libidinosas.
Y los claveles comenzaron a madurar brilloso
y las gardenias a eyacular coquetamente, muérete,
con sus durezas y blanduras y patas
y sangre amarilla, aj!
No se pare, no se siente, no hable
con la boca llena
de sangre:
que la sangre sueña con dalias
y las dalias empiezan a sangrar
y las palomas abortan cuervos   `
y claveles encinta
y unas magnolias curiosísimas, oye,
unas rosas re-raras, oh.

94

Conjurer's Tract

In the garden were some very curious magnolias, listen,
some really rare roses, oh,
and an awful smell of incest and blustery violets,
and semen flowing from hummingbird to hummingbird.
Then the girls came in the garden,
rain-soaked and full of white cockroaches,
and mayonnaise curdled in the kitchen
and their dolls began menstruating.
We caught you right in the act scrubbing pollen
off your skirt, nectar off your breasts, see?
Someone comes tip-toeing, a murmur of birds
being trampled, a skeleton being born in organza,
someone drew near in the middle of jokes and strawberries
and his grey hair waved green in the pool.
Tell me, you the one dead from laughter,
where you're taking that honeycomb of libidinous bees.
And carnations began blooming gloriously,
and gardenias ejaculating delightedly, die,
with their harshness and softness and paws
and yellow blood, ah!
Don't stand, don't sit, don't speak
with your mouth full
of blood:
let the blood dream of dahlias
and the dahlias begin bleeding
and the doves abort ravens
and pregnant carnations
and some very curious magnolias, hear,
some really rare roses, oh.